ANSWERS YOU NEED FOR

FLIP

BANK

LIVE

MIKE BAIRD & GREG HERLEAN

FLIP BANK LIVE
Answers You Need For Real Estate Profits

Mike Baird and Greg Herlean

Copyright © 2014 MG Success LLC
Cover photography (top, middle) by Josh Rossi

Published by MG LLC
2009 E Windmill Lane Las Vegas NV 89123
FlipBankLive.com

ISBN-10: 0991570529
ISBN-13: 978-0-9915705-2-2

Printed in the United States of America

ANSWERS YOU NEED FOR REAL ESTATE PROFITS

FLIP

BANK

LIVE

MIKE BAIRD & GREG HERLEAN

ACKNOWLEDGEMENTS

I would first like to thank my biggest cheerleader, my wife. You have been there for me since my very first investment property (which happened to be purchased on Valentine's Day). You have always listened to me and believed in me. Thank you for always keeping me focused on what is truly important in life.

To my five children, Elizabeth, Katelyn, Cassidy, Robert and Lucy, who would sit on the porch and watch me drive off to find a deal; I can still hearing you yelling "Go buy a house!" at the top of your lungs.

To my mom, thank you for taking the time to teach me everything good in this world, including poetry, music, hard work, honesty, morality, faith and love.

To my dad, you believed in me enough to buy me my first set of tools as a college graduation present. See what a $427 set of tools from Home Depot can do?! You taught me to be prudent and wise in all things. That advice has always steered me right.

To my Brothers of Baird Nation, David, John and Paul, you taught me what dreaming big and taking massive action is all about.

To my visionary grandmother, Lenore McNaughton, who told me-when I was a young college student: "If you don't invest in real estate while young, you are an IDIOT!" I'm glad that I took your advice.

To Danny Thompson, who was brave enough to document the destitute and unthinkable. Through your epic videography and teamwork, you have shown so many people across this nation exactly how neighborhoods are rebuilt.

And, lastly, many thanks to the thousands of houses, from mansions to meth homes, that seem to have whispered—and even yelled at times—specific and profitable lessons for success.

Mike Baird

ACKNOWLEDGEMENTS

I would like to personally acknowledge and thank my amazing friends. You have always supported me and been there whenever I needed you. I appreciate all of the time that you took for me and for the FaceTime calls, letters, cards and videos. I draw so much positive energy from you and that is what keeps me motivated. Much love!

To my team and partners: You allow me to learn and grow from the insight you share. I'm so grateful to have a team that always has my back. Jen, that means you, too. There is no way I could change lives, educate new investors and bring in profits for people all across this country without each and every one of you. My team is amazing.

To my beautiful children: You make everything worthwhile. You have given me so much joy and purpose in life. You know that I work hard so that I have more time to spend with you. Time is the most valuable thing we can offer up and I am grateful that I can spend so much of it with you. Carson, Colston, Maile and Cash: You are rock stars! At times, you are also a lot of work, ha!

Last, and certainly not least, a huge thanks to my wife, Kristy: You are my rock and my constant. I can always rely on your confidence in me. You make me want to be a better dad and husband. Kristy, you are truly my light and example. You constantly amaze me with all that you accomplish and how much love and care you infuse into our family. Love you!

Greg Herlean

THE *FLIP, BANK, LIVE.* PHILOSOPHY

Before you get started with this book, we wanted to take a moment to share the meaning behind Flip, Bank, Live. Flip, Bank, Live is more than just a book. It is a strategy that will show you how to obtain the lifestyle you want and deserve. Over the years, we have worked with many students who have attempted to start their real estate businesses without proper planning or a true strategy. We developed Flip, Bank, Live to ensure our students are always strategic and always focused on the end goal-to live well.

FLIP

The flipping stage is where most real estate investors start. Flipping is all about quick turnaround and quick money. It is active investing—hands-on and intense. Flipping is where you put in the most time and effort while absorbing as much knowledge and experience as possible. This is the stage where you begin to grow your business, capital and network of relationships.

BANK

The banking stage is where you graduate from active to passive investing. This is where you fund deals for other investors. This is where you free up your time and start to live the life you want on your own terms. In this stage, you are growing your passive investment portfolio and starting to remove yourself from the active tasks in your business. You are strategically placing your money into investments that will afford you a strong lifestyle for years to come.

LIVE

Living—living WELL—is both the end goal and the final stage. This is where all of your hard work and strategic planning pay off for you and your loved ones. The living stage is all about living the life you deserve: Working when you want to. Vacationing when you want to. Spending time with the charities and projects you care about. This is the stage where you are living your dream and giving back to your community.

INTRODUCTION

We wrote this book for one reason: to save you time and money!

This book contains the answers to questions that students and new investors ask us all the time. What we found is that these answers save people from falling into newbie investor mistakes that waste their time and eat into their profits.

We learned the answers to these questions through trial and error and now we are sharing that knowledge with you. We learned the hard way so you don't have to.

We love the real estate world. The money it brings. The changes it makes in communities. The freedom that it gives entrepreneurs and their families. The strength it brings to our country's economy. It is a wonderful industry. We are so happy that you have chosen to participate in this business. We welcome you to the club!

Remember that it may not always be easy but it will always be worth it.

Mike & Greg

STARTING YOUR REAL ESTATE BUSINESS

What advice would you give to someone who wants to get started in this business?

MIKE

The number one thing I recommend is for people to define what type of real estate investor they want to be. Do they want to be an active investor or do they want to be a passive investor? An active investor is one who is very hands-on. They are the ones out there finding properties. They are involved in the rehab and in the sale. An active investor seeks to make real estate their full-time profession. A passive investor is part-time. They can even be very, very part-time. For a passive investor, it is all about finding the right team to grow their investment dollars.

Because the types of deals you choose will vary, it is important that you make this decision upfront. Decide what parts of real estate you truly enjoy and how much time you have to dedicate to your real estate business. Doing this will save you a ton of time and energy and you will get started faster.

GREG

There are three points that I believe are crucial when getting started:

1. Be prepared to work harder than everyone else. Nothing rewards like hard work and dedication.

2. Get the right mindset. Challenges will come and you must be in the correct mindset to find solutions. Be ready for those challenges and never give up!

3. Model an expert. Find someone who is an expert in what you intend to do and get them to mentor you. You will excel faster and avoid common mistakes when you have a mentor.

What resources do I need to get involved in real estate?

MIKE

The most important resource to have right out of the gate is a clear understanding of market value. Market value is the price that an asset (or property) can be sold for in the market. If you can understand market value, you can earn a lot of money in the world of real estate. People make many mistakes when it comes to determining market value. They often neglect to understand that a property's market value is equal to what someone will pay for the property. It isn't subjective. It is all about the money that someone will put on the table to purchase. Understanding value will set you apart from the rest of the competition. It will also give you the ability to exploit markets and make a lot of money.

GREG

The most important resource that you can have when starting out in real estate is a solid and actionable deal-funding plan. You need a clear plan that lays out exactly how you are going to access the funds that you need to purchase, rehab and sell a property. Too many new investors start out by looking for deals. The truth is that the best deals are ones where you will have to act very quickly. If you wait until you find a deal to start looking for the money, you will find yourself losing many deals. That can get frustrating. So I tell everyone to start by getting your funding money in order and then finding deals that fit the resources you have available to you. Whether it is your own money or money you take on from investors, make sure you know what your deal-funding strategy is going to be before you even start looking for deals.

How much time do I need to put in each week to be successful in real estate?

MIKE

This depends on the type of investor you want to be. There are a lot of investors that are successful in this business with only part-time hours, 10-15 hours per week. Some even put in weekend hours only, when real estate activity tends to be busiest. Investors who finance deals for others typically put in only a few hours a month. It all comes down to the goals that investors want to set for themselves. Active investors, who are directly involved in the buying and selling of their properties, tend to be full-time, 30-50 hours per week. They need to put their full effort into managing properties and their progress.

GREG

As Mike says, you can put in as little or as much time as you want and still make money in real estate. The trick is to know how much time you want to put into your real estate investment business before you start. There are ways to make a lot of money in real estate, both actively and passively. I love lending to people who want to do all of the dirty work—finding, rehabbing and selling properties. For those that need or want to put in less time, being the bank, like me, is a fantastic option that requires little time. I love passive real estate profits. With trust deeds, I typically earn 8% to 10% doing absolutely nothing. I may initially put in three to five hours doing paperwork, but after that, I just collect checks.

What are the tax advantages associated with owning real estate?

MIKE

The first tax advantage that real estate investors find is in the setup of their real estate business entity. Most real estate investors set up a business themselves, perhaps an LLC or a C corporation. When you do so, you have all the advantages associated with business ownership and the deductions that come along with being a business owner (rents, equipment, etc.). Real estate also gives you a unique opportunity in terms of depreciation, which can be very, very big, especially as investors build long-term portfolios. There is also a deduction for the mortgage interest expense, which can reduce your tax burden significantly. A third benefit comes when you utilize self directed IRA accounts that allow you to grow your money tax-free. Real estate really is an investment vehicle that creates multiple tax advantages.

GREG

There are many advantages to real estate investment. The one I am most fond of sharing with others is the best tax advantage out there—tax-free profits! If you do your deals within a self directed IRA, you can pay nothing in taxes. That's a huge advantage! For those of you doing it outside of an SDIRA, another good tip is to hold the property for 12 months. When you do so, the profits from the deal are taxed as regular income, not as capital gains. This can get you a huge reduction in the amount of taxes you need to pay.

How involved do I have to be when rehabbing a property?

MIKE

The answer is specific to the individual. There are a lot of individual investors who do not want to go and see any of the properties. They do not want to be involved in the day-to-day work. Others really enjoy that process and enjoy seeing that transformation take place. Me, personally, I LOVE being a part of the rehabs. I love being able to create and to see properties go from A to Z. I love being the one who decides how to make things pretty. It is a very rewarding experience for me to see the transformation of a home, then a street, then an entire neighborhood. It gives me a great sense of accomplishment and pride to know that I was an active participant in that transformation. However, I realize that this is not the case for everyone. Those that don't want to get involved can hire professionals to provide those services for them.

GREG

I would say that you must be VERY involved in the beginning. This is where you can lose all of your potential profits if you aren't paying attention. When you are rehabbing a property, you must keep on top of every detail to make sure you are as profitable as possible. Now I am not saying that you have to do it yourself. What I am saying is that you need to make sure that you have eyes on your rehab projects every step of the way. If it is not you, make sure that the person you delegate this work to is really on top of every aspect of the rehab.

BUILDING A TEAM

How do I begin to assemble my team?

MIKE

First and foremost, people need to realize that the real estate business is the relationship business. Just like any other business out there, we focus on relationships. Relationships will make individuals more money than the deals themselves. So we want to be 100% relationship-minded from the get-go. To start, meet with real estate agents in your area. Attend meetings of real estate investors. While you are there, start building relationships and keep an eye out for the people that you might want to have on your team later

GREG

I started my first real estate team by finding two individuals who were already successful and getting them to allow me to follow their every move. I was willing to work for them. I started at the very bottom and worked my way up to the top. This allowed me to learn every aspect of the real estate business. I worked harder than anyone else. I started building my team by joining a successful, established team.

Who should be on my real estate team?

Who do you need to start building relationships with? My critical, first team members are real estate agents. They are seriously important. Most real estate investors make the mistake of not involving real estate agents. The majority of the deals I find come through real estate agent networks. After that, be sure to include a title company, general contractors, designers and financiers. Loan officers and private moneylenders are critical resources that you can tap to get access to money quickly.

For me, the critical, core team members on a real estate team are:

- A bird dog to find your properties

- A rehab team

- A project manager

- A financial manager

- A title company

How do I know which contractor to hire?

MIKE

References. Take the time to get references. Take the time to go and see the work that has been done by these contractors. Talk to the clients of these contractors and get their feedback. The next thing you want to do is get multiple bids. Find multiple contractors and get them together. Give them all the same information about the work that you need done. Then, have them all bid on the same scope of work. This ensures you can perform an apples-to-apples comparison of the bids. Get a feel for their respective areas of expertise and for the types of work they like to do. Contractors are notorious for saying they know how to do everything. I like to find contractors who are masters of their specific craft. When you have a contractor who does work in an area where they are exceptional, the project will come out 100% better. Your buyers will appreciate that.

GREG

You should only hire contractors who can provide multiple referrals. Call those referrals and find out how satisfied they were overall. One thing I always make sure to ask each reference is how the contractor handled challenges. You are looking for answers that indicate that the contractor was quick to report issues or challenges and that the contractor also brought solutions to address those challenges. Contractors who truly know their stuff are prepared for the unexpected. They understand how to work around surprises. They should be bringing you solutions, not just issues.

GETTING
STARTED

What can I expect during my first few months in the real estate business?

MIKE

The first few months of your business have to be focused on developing your team. You need to be developing the relationships with the individuals who are going to give you the ability to get deals done. During the first couple of months, you also need to be focused on understanding value and identifying the neighborhoods where you feel comfortable. I find that identifying the area—and then building relationships with people who are experts in that area—is a true recipe for success. That is how offers get made and deals can be had.

GREG

The first thing I tell new investors is that you will not make huge money on your first few deals. Sorry, you just won't. BUT you will learn the things that will make or save you huge money later on. The second thing I tell new investors is to expect that you will make mistakes.

The most important thing is that you get started. Don't get held up focusing on the small things. Start doing and start learning.

How do I know what area to invest in?

MIKE

The most important thing is to start with an area that you know very well. These are most likely the areas that you frequently drive through. Perhaps you walk or ride your bike through these areas as well. I say this because these are the areas that you are already familiar with. You know the clientele. You know the type of people that already live there. You know if the area is on an upswing or a downswing. You know if people are moving in or out of these areas. You know if the area has an appreciating market. Pick a neighborhood that you already know when you are first starting out. Take the time to familiarize yourself with every aspect of that area. Make sure that the neighborhood has a stable real estate market and that the people who live there display pride of ownership.

GREG

I always tell people to invest in the area that you know best. Don't start with a flip in an unknown town. That can spell trouble. As you mature in your real estate experience, you will be able to do deals in areas that are far from where you live. However, do your first deal in your own backyard, where you already know the market and the area. This will allow you to gain a deep understanding of everything involved in a flip. You will need this knowledge when you do branch out to other areas.

How do I decide what price point to invest in?

.

MIKE

I have a very simple rule of thumb:

Investors should invest in properties with values at the median price point for the area in which they are choosing to do business.

In every neighborhood across the country, the majority of transactions that take place occur at the median value level. So when you have a home that is at that median price point, you greatly increase your sale opportunities. Whenever you go into higher price points for a given area, there are fewer buyers and properties sit longer. Remember that when you are just coming out of the gate, speed is your best friend. In order to get that speed, your sales need to target the most active set of buyers for the area. Those buyers are all looking toward the median price point.

GREG

My answer goes hand-in-hand with my advice to know how you are funding your deals upfront: invest at whatever price point you feel comfortable risking your funds. There are going to be times when you find a fantastic deal on a home that might be outside the price point you originally targeted. My sweet spot for single-family homes is the $150,000 to $500,000 range, depending on the neighborhood and what houses in the neighborhood are currently selling for.

Where should my focus be when I start?

Getting Started

MIKE

This is going to depend on your goals. If you are interested in flipping homes, then the focus should be on those median price point properties. Homes where there is a lot of activity. Homes that can be bought and sold quickly.

If individuals are looking for long-term holds, they are going to be more interested in terms. Where are the terms going to make sense? It may not be as important to understand these areas so thoroughly when we are working a quick flip. We are not going to be as price-sensitive in these areas. We are going to be term-sensitive, which means to be sensitive to the monthly cash flow of the property. What is my debt service going to be? What is my monthly rental income going to be? What type of tenant can I attract in that specific area? Can I attract long-term, dependable tenants to this property?

GREG

Your focus should be on the acquisition of knowledge. You may not make very much money during your first few deals, but the knowledge you gain will make and save you millions as a real estate investor. Spend your early days learning from the experienced people that you bring onto your team. This will help you build a strong knowledge base for future profits.

What are some of the common pitfalls
that I need to watch out for?

MIKE

The most common mistake that real estate investors make is to get overly emotional about a property. They get so attached and excited that they ignore the fundamentals of the deal. I have seen the most well-prepared and intelligent investors lose sight of the end goal—the profit—when they allow emotion to come into play. They make mistakes like overpaying for a property or adding in rehab extras when they should not. When your emotions come into play, take a deep breath and step back. Take a moment to review your plans and your criteria. Then, ask yourself, does this property fit your criteria? Is this decision going to give you the profits you need on this property? The answers are simple yes or no answers and they will tell you what you need to do. Do the math and don't get emotional.

GREG

One of the most common mistakes I see is when investors get so excited about the property they do not stop and ensure that there is a clean title on the property. Not having a clean title can get you into a lot of trouble.

The other thing that I always point out is you should always insure a property right away. The unexpected can happen at any moment. Don't take a risk. Get it insured.

Should I get my real estate license?

MIKE

While I wouldn't say that getting your real estate license is required on the first day, it is something that I believe can prove valuable as a real estate investor. I refer to this as adding a tool to your toolbox. The more tools you have in your toolbox, the better off you will be. So either you need to get your real estate license or you need to have a person with a license on your team. Note that this team member should be someone who is intimately involved with your business and has your interests in mind. The most valuable tool a real estate agent with a license will provide for you is information. Information is power, especially when it comes to evaluating properties. I like to have as many tools as possible in my toolbox when I go into the marketplace. So either I am going to have a license or I am going to have someone on my team with a license.

GREG

I actually do not recommend that people jump at getting a real estate license. I prefer to bring on a team member who has one. I want to stay focused on other aspects of my business, like the money and profits. The real estate agent is a critical component of the team and I feel that someone who is solely dedicated to that task is the best one to handle it. Start flipping and lending first. Add a licensed real estate agent to your team. Wait awhile and then decide if you actually want to pursue a license or continue to let someone else on your team handle it.

Should I get my mortgage license?

MIKE

No. The mortgage industry is constantly changing. Guidelines, regulations and product offerings are always in flux. Knowledge in this industry is something that you have to familiarize yourself with on a daily basis. As a real estate investor, especially if you want to be one who is actively involved in your flips, you don't want to take this on. It will take away your focus and you will never be as adept at finding the right loans as a dedicated mortgage professional will. This is an area where I will have more than one source for originating loans so I can do deals back-to-back, without delay.

GREG

No. Just like a real estate agent's license, there is no need to get a mortgage license. This is another position on the team that I fill with someone who is fully committed to this area. Having a licensed mortgage broker on your team is critical. I say "broker" because they will be able to source multiple loans at once and find you the most favorable terms on every deal. This is something you definitely do not jump into. If, after awhile, you decide that you absolutely want to do this, you can. But I believe you will find that a mortgage broker is someone you want on your team, not a title you want to pursue.

What sort of licensed credentials should I get?

MIKE

Legally speaking, you do not need any licenses to be a full-time real estate investor. However, some of these licensed credentials will save you money and give you access to resources that can be a huge asset to your business. In my opinion, the two most important license credentials to obtain are a real estate license and a general contractor license. The reason is because each real estate transaction that you are involved in will include large fees for the agent and general contractor. Having you or someone on your team with these licensed credentials can prove to be very valuable.

GREG

While I do agree with Mike that there are some benefits to holding specific licenses, I definitely feel that this is something you should not be concentrating on at all in the beginning. This is a common mistake people make. They spend time getting licenses before they even know what they want to do with their real estate investing. Make money first! Decide later whether or not you want a particular license.

What is the most important thing I should have before I start my real estate investing business?

MIKE

First and foremost, you have to have education and know-how. Understand what principles govern the real estate market and how you want to play in that marketplace.

The second thing you need is a desire to learn and a desire to go out and gather information. A lot of that information is going to come through the team that you create. So create a team that will support you and provide that market information.

The third thing you need is the ability to go out and understand a marketplace—what it's doing, what the price points are, what factors are affecting the value of properties in that area, what you can do to increase value in the short-term and what you need to do to properly manage assets for the long-term. When you have the answers to those questions, you will make good decisions when deciding on investments.

GREG

The two things that I would say you need to have when you get started in real estate investing are a money plan and the right frame of mind. Your money plan will help you understand what type of investments will give you the returns you are seeking. It will tell you what types of investments offer those returns and which are the ones that you should pursue. It will tell you where you are going to get the money to go after those very deals. In my opinion, it is the most important business plan an investor can have.

The second is the right frame of mind. Look, I know that it might not be what you want to hear, but it may be hard in the beginning. If you aren't ready to attack with your plan and deal with challenges, don't start yet. Start your investing from a position of strength.

What should I do to prepare before I buy my first home?

MIKE

Before you do anything else, get your financial house in order. This involves meeting with a loan officer. You should know what your spending limit is before you start evaluating deals. Remember that the best deals will move quickly. Be ready for that. When you are just starting out, investors and banks will be looking at your personal credit. Make sure that your credit score is in good shape. Also, for those of you who are heading into real estate investment as a full-time career, make sure that you have some personal reserves set aside to carry you through your first few deals. If you do not do this, you will make poor decisions on your flips and ruin your chances. You can prevent this by taking the pressure off of yourself ahead of time.

GREG

The best thing you can do for yourself to ensure profit is to understand every component of the deal you are about to execute. Know what is required to acquire the property, to rehab the property and to sell the property. Make sure that you have the funds to cover every phase of the investment. Always make sure you know how much money you are going to make on the deal when it is done. Be realistic with your profit expectations. Lastly, before a single hammer is swung, get to know every member of your rehab team. Your profit is in their hands.

FINDING A DEAL

How do I find out what is owed on a property?

The best source for finding out what is owed on a property is a search of the public records for a property. These records are sometimes available online. You will need to check the city or county clerk's office covering the property. Many cities and counties still require that you physically visit their offices to perform the record search.

That said, I prefer to use title companies. Title companies specialize in providing this information. This is one reason why creating a strong relationship with a title company is important. This is often your best source for finding the most up to date title information.

How do I beat out the competition with my offers?

To beat out the competition, you either have to be the first offer in or the last offer that is submitted and signed.

When you are the first offer, you are counting on speed and a seller that needs to sell the property fast. I say "need" because when individuals need to sell a property, they will often take the first strong offer that comes in.

When you are the last, you are competing with other offers and you must have a feel for where those other offers might be in terms of price. The biggest points that you are going to want to negotiate are price and terms. For example, a seller may receive two offers for a property that both offer $100,000. However, one offer will put up $5,000 earnest money that is refundable while the second offers to make a non-refundable earnest money deposit. They are willing to put the money up "hard," so to speak. The seller is likely to take the second offer because the second buyer is demonstrating that they are committed to getting the deal done, so much so that they will lose their deposit money if the sale does not go through. Another tactic to win in a last bid scenario is to remove contingencies from the sale in your offer. For example, bringing all cash to a deal will remove the loan contingency, which is very favorable to sellers. Ultimately, you are looking for any competitive advantage you can offer that will get the deal accepted and closed quickly.

I hear a lot about foreclosure auctions, are these viable places to buy property?

Yes, you can buy good deals at foreclosure auctions. However, foreclosure auctions across the country are getting very, very, very competitive. It can be difficult and dangerous to buy here. The danger comes from the imperfect information that is often provided for the properties at auction. That said, this poor flow of information is also what provides the opportunity.

I do not recommend that novice investors buy properties at foreclosure auctions simply because the risks are so high and novices are not ready for such great risk. They need more knowledge and experience first. There are liens. There are encumbrances. There is heavy competition. It will be a very difficult and frustrating purchase for someone who is just starting out.

How do I find REO properties? Are these a good source for finding potential investment properties?

REO properties are Real Estate-Owned properties. They are also known as bank-owned properties. Banks receive these properties following a foreclosure sale. In the event that a property goes to foreclosure and is not purchased by a third party at the foreclosure sale, the bank takes ownership of the property.

These properties are typically listed through real estate agents who specialize in REO listings. The properties will be listed in the Multiple Listing Service (MLS). While these are good sources for finding property, I encourage people to focus on the relationship that they have with these REO real estate agents during these transactions. Your relationship with the REO agent is just as important as getting the property you are inquiring about.

Can I find good deals with short sales?

Yes, there are many good deals found in short sales, but they often require a high level of patience with the bank that is holding the notes for the property. Banks are notorious for having very slow response times during a short sale offer. You have to realize that the foreclosure and the short sale offer typically occur at the same time. The bank will be trying to simultaneously get the loan in good standing while it is entertaining short sale offers. If you are patient and have the time to wait for the bank to accept your short sale offer, you will find some really good deals.

Should I buy a home from a Trustee Sale?

Trustee sales can be a great place to buy, but they are also a dangerous place to buy. Most people don't even realize that when they go to a trustee sale, they are not actually buying a property. They are buying a deed of trust.

This means that there is a loan or a debt associated with that property. That debt on the property is what is known as a title description. You are essentially buying that title description. Trustee sales can be profitable because the imperfect information there provides that opportunity. However, these sales can have a lot of competition and the experiences of the investor after the purchase can be very frustrating for the buyer. Those that have the stomach and the financial ability to buy property at a trustee sale on a consistent and continual basis can do very well. This is certainly not a starting point.

How do I deal with the red tape often associated with HUD and REO homes?

First, you have to accept the fact that there is a lot of red tape associated with these types of properties simply because you are dealing with large financial institutions. They are bound by rules and regulations and often imperfect processes. However, they must follow these processes to the letter in order to clear title on the property so that they can be sold quickly. The easiest way to work through the red tape is to hire a real estate agent who does a lot of transactions with those types of properties. They will understand the paperwork, know the institutional process and know what the institutions like to see. Utilizing an agent who specializes in these types of homes will greatly increase your chances of getting your offers accepted. Meet with a professional who deals with HUD and REO properties on a regular basis. Having him or her on your team will prove valuable.

How do I know that the deal I found is a good deal?

One of the very first things that I encourage students to do is to gain a true understanding of value. They need to know what a specific property will sell for in a specific area at a specific time. Once you know what a property will sell for, you can then work backwards to analyze and lock in a guaranteed profit. The key is to understand what the value of the property is on the day you buy it and to know specifically what rehab you should do to drive that value up significantly. You then build in your carrying costs and the profit you want. At that point, when you know all of your figures, if the cost of acquiring the property is lower, then you know you have a good deal.

When Market Value > (Purchase Price + Rehab Costs + Holding Costs + Desired Profit), you have a winner.

BASIC
DEAL-FUNDING
QUESTIONS

Why are banks not lending to me or others?

Banks are lending, but not quickly enough. Most banks will lend money to a borrower with good credit (a credit score above 700) and a W-2 paying job for properties that are already finished and in good condition. If you do not meet those qualifications, then your loan may take 60-120 days to go though. The problem with depending on traditional financing for investment properties is that most investment deals need to close in 30 days or less. Even the most qualified candidates are seeing that their loans are taking much longer than that.

What kind of credit score do I need to get
a loan for an investment property?

If you are going to go to a bank for a loan on an investment property, you should have a score above 680. If you seek out private investment, your credit score may not be the most important factor for the private lender. Private lenders tend to scrutinize the deal much more closely than they scrutinize the borrower's personal credit. They are looking at whether or not the deal is a profitable one.

What are the best ways for me to fund my deal?

There are many, many ways to fund a deal. I am going to share with you how I did it. I started with no money and worked my way up from there. I started by utilizing self directed IRAs. These vehicles allow you to utilize your own self directed retirement accounts or to leverage someone else's. (Come to my event and learn how!)

Another way to fund a deal is through the use of what I refer to as the Infinite Banking Concept. You can lend yourself funds from your insurance policy. No, not all insurance policies will allow you to borrow against them, but there are those that will. This is a way for you to keep your money liquid while at the same time growing your money tax-free.

Another method is to leverage the funds of hard money and private lenders.

And, finally, cash always works.

How can I use my retirement account to fund my deal?

This is by far my favorite method of funding a deal and also the one that I started with. There are four easy steps to funding your deal with your retirement account:

- Open a self directed retirement account with an SDIRA custodian. One of my companies, Horizon Trust (HorizonTrust. com), is an SDIRA custodian

- Transfer funds from your existing IRA or 401(k) into that new self directed account. If you have not made your annual contribution, you can also add that to your new account.

- Once your account is open, direct your custodian to fund your deal.

- Done! Your IRA now owns the deal and your profits are sheltered by the tax advantages of the account.

How can I use my life insurance to fund my deal?

The fundamentals are quite simple.

- You take out a whole life policy that allows you to put money into the account that will grow tax-free.

  - Note that you are looking at policies that allow you to utilize the highest amount of cash contributions over those that offer the highest death benefits. You need to make sure that you select the right type of policy to utilize this investment method.

- You can then borrow against the money and take it out to fund your deals.

For a deeper explanation, please see the video posted on my site: http://www.bankonthis.com/becomethebank/

Should I use one or multiple money sources?

You should always have a list of four to five resources that you can go to when you need funding. As I have said before, these deals tend to move quickly. As such, you need to have multiple funding options so that you are not constrained and can access funds rapidly enough to get the deal funded. This is essential because there will be many times when a funding source may not be able to work with your timeline. Having additional options ensures that you are always covered and always ready to act.

What terms should I offer a private lender when borrowing money to fund my deal?

There are many, many combinations of terms that can be offered to a hard money lender or private investor. That said, most are a combination of annual interest and/or a percentage of the profits from the deal. You will need to find a combination of the two that is most attractive to the lender.

- There is usually an interest rate on the money. With hard money or private investors, this rate is typically 10% to 14% annually plus 1% to 4% in origination fees. These loans are typically set to last for the duration of 12 months.

- There may also be a percentage of profit shares, where the lender requests a share of the profits from the deal in lieu of, or in addition to, the interest on the money loaned. Typically, the percentage of profit to the lender falls between 20% and 80%. The percentage of profit will be impacted by the other loan terms you agree to. For example, a lender may agree to a very low interest rate (or none at all) in exchange for 70% of the profits. I recommend attempting profit split deals when you first start out. This allows you to avoid the pressure of accumulating interest costs as you do your first few deals. It gives you the flexibility you need in the beginning.

How do I pull in money partners?

Basic Deal-Funding Questions

Pulling in money partners is all about information and presentation. You need to know what you want and what you have to offer in exchange before you get in front of any investor. Going into any conversation with a potential investor without clearly being able to identify what you need in order to deliver profits to them is a recipe for disaster. You need to make it clear and simple. You need to be able to answer questions. Being able to provide clear and definitive information shows that you know what you are doing and that you will not waste their time or money. Do not act desperate or like a first-timer. They will sense it.

Talk to other real estate investors in your area and find out whom they are using to fund their deals. They are everywhere. Remember, too, that IRA owners are also everywhere. They have money in their retirement accounts that is just sitting there. I look at the 79 million IRA holders in the U.S. as my potential money partners.

How do I find money to invest in a house when I have never done a deal?

The answer to this question is in the team that you build. This is another reason that it is critical for you to bring experienced people onto your team. Of course, you are going to lack experience in the beginning, but you are not doing the deals yourself. You and your team are doing them. Leverage the experience of your team. Utilize the word "we."

How did you structure your first deal?

Basic Deal-Funding Questions

My very first deal was actually quite simple and it is a structure that I recommend to anyone who is starting out. Did I make a ton of money on my first few deals? No, I didn't. And that is why I tell you that you are not going to either. That is NOT a bad thing. It is experience and knowledge that you are after. To fund my first deal, my private lender put up 100% of all the costs (to acquire and rehab the property). In return, I secured their money with a lien on the property and gave them 75% of the profits. I did all of the work required and walked away with 25% of profits on a deal that I had no money in.

How do I market to hard money or private money lenders?

As I said before, you need to find out who is lending in your area today and reach out to those people when you have a deal. When you present a deal to a potential money source, I recommend that you have a clear summary you can leave them with.

After you complete your first successful deal, you can turn your project into a one- or two-page summary and send it to all of the lenders in your area without asking anything from them. Then, when you have your next deal, they will already know that you have had success and will be more likely to take a meeting with you.

Are hard money loans riskier than the bank loans offered by traditional lending institutions?

No. In fact, sometimes it's actually the opposite. How? Well, hard money lenders will frequently insist that the borrower put more skin in the game. They may require the borrower to bring 30% to 50% at closing. This is how they mitigate their risk. Banks, on the other hand, are frequently satisfied with 5% to 10% down from the borrower. The borrower has a lot less skin in the game under those circumstances. When a bank focuses solely on the credit score and the W-2 information of a borrower, they often neglect to see that the focus really should be on the value of the property and the profit to be made in the deal. A hard money lender takes that very approach. They recognize that the value is in the deal itself and in the collateral. They will lend only when the borrower commits to the deal with a larger down payment. This lessens the risk of the borrower defaulting.

REAL ESTATE
PRIVATE INVESTMENT

How do I lend to real estate investors while making sure my money is safe?

I strongly recommend that you use a professional company who is focused on vetting the deals. This should be the primary way that they make their own profits. Please do not try to do your own lending in the beginning. A mortgage broker/banker does this for a living. Working with one of them will not only mitigate your risk, it will also allow you to learn a lot. You will start to see what critical factors you should consider when evaluating a deal that is presented to you. Using a mortgage broker/banker to find your deals can help you save hundreds of thousands of dollars. Be careful here. I have seen many people try to eliminate the middle-man, but all they end up doing is losing all of their money because it was not done right and was underwritten incorrectly. Let me also stress that you must use a title company to execute your deals. You need to make sure that title is free and clear before proceeding with any property.

How can I become the bank?

Basic Deal-Funding Questions

You can become the bank by using your money to lend to real estate investors. As I said previously, be sure to use a mortgage broker/banker when you first start out. As you get more experienced, you may be able to evaluate deals on your own. When that happens, my advice is to always make sure that you are in first position on the property. You want to make sure that you have the best standing possible just in case things go awry. I want to also point out that you should not lend out money that you need to live. This is why I am fond of utilizing IRA money to fund real estate deals. IRA money is money that I am growing and saving for retirement. It is not money that I expect to be liquid today.

What is the minimum amount of money that I need to have ready to get started with the banking concept?

You can start lending money when you have as little as $10,000. The more you have to lend, the more profitable a deal you can construct, but you can begin with very little.

It is important to remember that having money to invest doesn't necessarily mean having $10,000 cash in your checking account. Make sure that as you assess your funding options, you take a look at any existing retirement and insurance accounts that you have. You may be able to self direct your IRA and use those funds to become the bank. The same may be true of a life insurance policy if you have the right plan.

Why should I learn this when I already
have a financial advisor?

You don't have to have me! Nor do you have to have a financial advisor. Financial advisors typically can only show you traditional marketable securities. They cannot show you alternative investments, such as real estate, businesses, gold, etc. Why? Well, because they don't make money when they show you those types of deals. They are focused on traditional securities because that is where they make their money.

However, I am in no way advising you to move all of your money away from your financial advisor. I recommend that you start with a portion of your investment funds. Then, compare the returns you are getting from your traditional securities with your real estate and business investments. As you get more comfortable with your alternative investments, you can make the decision to move more of your portfolio that way if it makes you more money.

What documents are needed in a deal where I am the bank and lending my money?

To fund a real estate deal as the bank, the following documents will be required to close the deal. There may be additional documents, depending upon the state in which the property exists, but these are the fundamental ones:

- Mortgage License Division (MLD) disclosure statements. All general disclosures required for all loans in your state

- Loan-specific MLD disclosures.

- Executed and notarized Power of Attorney (POA).

- Executed Loan Summary.

- Executed Loan Servicing Agreement.

- Executed Investor Escrow Instructions.

- Executed MLD Receipt of Documents.

- If investor is purchasing with qualified funds, an executed Direction of Investment (DOI) form.

- Executed Sharing of Investor Information form.

SELF DIRECTED ACCOUNTS

What are typical IRA custodial fees?

While each custodial company will have its own fee schedule, you will find that the fees are all about the same. Some will have a lower annual fee but larger transactional costs. Or they will charge a larger annual fee but include many of the transaction fees that you might find with other custodians. The bottom line is that these fees, no matter how they are structured, will still be much lower than the ones you will encounter from a financial advisor who is managing your money. In almost any scenario, you will likely be paying half of what you are paying with a financial advisor. What you are really looking for is great customer service. You are looking for a company that is responsive and tends to your needs quickly and effectively. I invite you to take a look at my company Horizon Trust. If you choose Horizon Trust, mention this book and I will waive your set up fee.

Another point to mention is that your annual fee is a tax write-off if you pay it outside of your IRA.

Is the banking strategy you describe available for my RRSP Funds?

While there are ways to use your RRSP in specific provinces to invest in real estate, it is a complicated process and can be quite cumbersome. For our Canadian investors, we recommend that you execute cash transactions.

How much can I contribute to my IRA each year?

Let me first point out that an annual contribution is the amount of new money that you are allowed to put into your IRA account each year. However, once the money is in your account, there is no limit on your money's growth. For example, you may contribute up to $5,500 each year to your Roth account. You can grow that money into $10,000 or $100,000 tax-free.

For the 2014 tax year, you may contribute up to $5,500 to a traditional or Roth IRA. This amount is $6,500 annually if you are age 50 or older. You may contribute up to $50,000 each year to an individual 401(k) plan.

These amounts change every few years. The contribution limits are always available on www.irs.gov.

TRUST DEEDS

How can I use my self directed IRA to purchase trust deeds?

It is quite easy. Once your self directed IRA is opened with your custodian, you will ask your custodian for a direction to invest form. This form is what you will complete to execute any transaction, be it an investment in a trust deed or a business. This form tells the custodian what you are instructing them to do with your funds. When the investment starts paying your returns, they will be paid directly back into your self directed account.

Why do I need a trust deed broker when I already have a financial advisor?

These two professionals play very different roles in your investment career. The financial advisor makes money by telling you where to put your money, typically mutual funds and annuities that they are being paid to sell. The other professional, the mortgage broker, makes money by identifying and performing due diligence on real estate deals and the underlying assets. The mortgage broker's primary responsibility is to evaluate, underwrite and legally execute solid real estate deals.

If you haven't guessed by now, I feel that a mortgage broker is key to identifying the deals that will bring you solid and secure monthly returns. I learned at a very young age that financial advisors are not in the deals their investors make and they are not there to protect their investors. They are there for commissions. I prefer to work with professionals who are in the deal with me and whose primary focus is on ensuring that I make secure and predictable investments.

Why should I invest in trust deeds instead of what I am doing now?

I am a huge advocate of becoming the bank and becoming a trust deed investor. It is the best way that I have found to invest in real estate without much work. Real estate is what I believe in and that is why I choose to fund real estate deals as the bank. This is what I have made my money doing so it shouldn't surprise anyone that this is the advice I would give to any other investor. I have found trust deed investments to be more stable and predictable than the stock market. Furthermore, I prefer to use what I know to evaluate the deals that I put my money into. I do not want a junior analyst telling me that 2% annually should make me happy. Once you learn this business, you will understand exactly what I am saying.

When will I start receiving interest payments?

The answer to this question is in the terms of your lending agreement. What I recommend is that you ensure that you are receiving monthly checks. I tend to reject terms where principal and interest payments are offered on a quarterly or annual basis. I want to see steady payments coming in each month. These monthly payments typically start 30 days after the loan is closed.

How long do trust deeds typically last?

Again, this depends on the terms of the trust deed itself. Some can have terms as short as three months, others five years. That said, my sweet spot for trust deed duration is between 12 and 24 months. Typically, the trust deeds I choose are set up for 12 or 18 months with only one or two six-month extensions available. One of the things I like most about trust deed investments is that they are not long-term. I recommend that you select trust deeds that meet the criteria I just described.

Can I lose my money in trust deeds?

I know that you want the answer to be no, but that is not the case. As with any investment, you can lose money on a trust deed. However, I find trust deed investments to be safer than other investments out there, such as stocks or investing in businesses. I will point out that losing money on a trust deed is mitigated because it is collateralized with actual real estate. When you choose a good mortgage broker to identify solid trust deed investments for you, you will select from trust deed investments that have been properly vetted and executed. This protects you by ensuring that both the property and the borrower are solid investments. Furthermore, should an issue arise where the borrower is unable to pay back the loan, the mortgage broker will execute the foreclosure and resale process on behalf of their investors. They will take control of the property legally and secure the rights of the investors. This is why you should select a solid trust deed mortgage broker to fortify your investments.

What is a second deed of trust?

A second deed of trust is a loan that is in second position on a property. It comes after a first deed of trust. People frequently think that a second deed of trust means that it is a weak position. This is not always the case. For example, let's say that a borrower defaulted on a million dollar property. The property must be taken back and sold to return the funds to those who are carrying the first and second deeds of trust. Should you be scared if you are an investor on the second deed of trust?

It depends. If the property is worth $1 million and the first trust deed is for $300,000 and the second is for $100,000, then no, you shouldn't be scared. In the event of default, the property sale will likely take care of both the first and the second. That is why you need to look at each deal. I strongly prefer to invest in first trust deeds, but have invested in seconds many times. It's all about evaluating the risk and the returns.

Why haven't any of my friends, family members or colleagues heard of this?

It isn't taught in schools. I'm not trying to be sarcastic. I am being quite serious when I say real financial education—as in, how to grow wealth—just isn't taught in schools. It's something you have to learn on your own. Think back to when Mitt Romney was running for president and everyone was shocked by the size of his multimillion-dollar retirement accounts. Newspapers even wrote articles questioning how that was even possible! It was ridiculous. Not only did he build his self directed IRA legally and effectively, every single working American can do the exact same thing. The only reason that they don't know how is because no ever taught them.

I say that you need to educate the people you care for and share this knowledge you have with them. That is my mission and that is what drives me. Share what you know and improve their lives.

What secures a trust deed?

The property is what secures a trust deed. It really is that simple. Sometimes, there may be additional collateral on a trust deed. In addition to the property that the loan is being made on, the borrower may put up additional collateral. Typically, though, the loan is collateralized by the subject property.

REAL ESTATE REHAB

What are the most expensive problems to solve during a rehab project?

The most expensive problems to solve are always going to be foundational or structural in nature. If those types of issues are not resolved properly through licensed general contractors, the potential for profit in that particular property is ZERO. That said, sometimes the most expensive property to rehab can be the most profitable. If those expenses are properly understood and taken into consideration when you are buying the property, then the deal can be very profitable.

I do NOT recommend these types of deals for investors who are just starting. The risks are too great.

What is the most important room in a
house when you are rehabbing it?

The most important room in the house is 100%, without a doubt, the kitchen. The kitchen and the family rooms are the heart and center of a home. People love to entertain. They love to make memories there. We find over and over again that kitchens done right will sell a home. You need to have kitchens with a little bit of zing. Stainless steel appliances, granite countertops, a nice backsplash and great light fixtures will set a kitchen apart and sell a house faster.

Do light fixtures and doorknobs really matter?

Absolutely! When buyers enter your home, they are looking for specific details that show them the house has quality. It has to be a place where they want to live, a place where they want to create memories. Things like doorknobs, hardware, cabinetry and light fixtures are items that I refer to as "house jewelry." Think of them as accessories for a home's outfit. Buyers notice these details and appreciate them. They are willing to pay a premium to rehabbers who pay attention to these specific details. Those little details will set you and your home apart from the rest of the competition.

How do you get a lawn to turn green fast?

Oftentimes, when we buy a property through distressed means, yards have gone to the pits! They look like junkyards. Don't despair! There is a trick to turning that brown yard into a green lawn. It is a chemical known as ammonium sulfate. When you dust dead grass with ammonium sulfate, your lawn will be green again in three to seven days.

What are your favorite paint colors?

My favorite paint colors are neutral, which is attractive to the majority of potential buyers. This doesn't automatically mean white, despite what many first-time rehabbers think. This just means colors that work like flexible canvases so different people with various styles can impart their design touches. Some colors used recently include cream and cooler grays. In the past, very natural tan tones have been used. However, over the past several years, creams and grays have proven very appealing to homebuyers.

How do I know if I should take down a wall or leave it alone?

Opening space to create larger spaces is something that buyers are willing to pay for. It is what they are looking for. As a rehabber, it is a common desire, but a difficult decision must be made. It can be difficult to determine whether or not a wall is structurally bearing. I recommend getting a licensed general contractor into the home to examine the wall you are considering taking down to determine whether or not the wall is load bearing.

In the event that it is not load bearing, feel free to bring out your sledgehammer. Taking down a wall is a great way to open up a space and make a room look larger. Even when the wall turns out to be load bearing, the possibility of removing it is not lost. If you really want to remove the wall, you just need to work with your contractor to make sure that the necessary structural support is put in elsewhere. When you do take down a structural wall, you should always get a letter and a plan from an engineer or general contractor to have the work done properly.

How many bids should I get before
picking a contractor to do the work?

I always get at least three bids before selecting a contractor. This is very important: the cheapest bid is not always the correct one. Pick the bid that offers the best combination of timeline and project plan from a competent contractor. It is very important to speak with at least three contractors with good references. You need to analyze their work and their experience. Make your decision based on those factors.

SELLING
THE
PROPERTY

How do you know what your house is going to sell for?

The easiest answer to this question lies in the sales of similar properties in the marketplace you are working. Those are referred to as comparable sales, or comps for short. If the subject property is 2,000 square feet, I would go into the marketplace and find homes that are similar in size, age and style. I would analyze their condition against the subject property. By comparing against homes that have actually sold, I have a good idea what my property is worth. Remember that any investment is only worth what someone is willing to actually pay for it and that you do not make money until the property is sold.

Some first-time investors try to use active listings to determine the value of their property. This is absolutely incorrect. Only use data from properties that have actually sold. Data from properties that have sold in the last 60-90 days are best.

Are real estate agents worth the money?

I have met hundreds of real estate agents that I feel are not worth a cent. I know that sounds a little brutal, but it is true. Oftentimes, I wonder how these people even managed to get a license. That type of agent is what I refer to as "hype." On the other hand, there are many agents I would pay a handsome fee to because they have extensive experience and value-add. I regularly seek out agents who have knowledge and connections within my markets. I bring them onto my team and work closely with them. They understand value. They understand what homes will sell for. And they have your best interests in mind.

Is staging worth the time and money?

Staging is absolutely worth your time, money and energy. One of my biggest secrets is that my homes sell faster and for more money because of the way I stage them. All of my direct competitors are now trying to do the same thing. Why? Because it works! I couldn't be a bigger fan of staging.

We want potential buyers entering our homes to be able to picture themselves in the home. We want them to imagine themselves creating memories there. We do not want them thinking about how much the house was bought for or what color they need to repaint the walls. These are the things that people tend to think of when a home is empty or not staged right. Staging turns a house into a home and will get you the money you deserve.

Should I flip a house quickly or should I hold for the long term?

This really depends on what your goals are. If you are looking to make some quick money in the next 90 days, then flipping a property is for you. If you are thinking about holding onto the property for the long term and creating a rental portfolio, obviously you need to move towards getting a property rent-ready with the right tenant. It is important to note that good flip properties are not always good rental properties and vice versa. On flips, I focus on price. On long-term rentals, I focus on long-term cash flow and the terms of the deal that will provide me with that cash flow.

What rate of return can I expect on a short-term (flip) investment?

Investors right now are shooting for a 15% to 25% return on their money for flips. This is not an annual return. This is the return for a specific property. If I were to invest $100,000 on a property, I would expect to make $15,000 to $25,000 when it is sold and all expenses are paid. Those rates of return do tend to fluctuate.

When markets are hot and there are a lot of transactions taking place, the rates of return tend to decrease. That said, in a hot market, you tend to turn transactions over faster and so will earn smaller returns more often. The numerous smaller transactions can add up to quite a large sum. When there are fewer players in the marketplace and there is less competition, those rates of return can be much higher. Unlike a hot market, the rates of return here may be higher, but you tend to do fewer transactions.

What rate of return can I expect on a long-term (hold) investment?

Investors in today's marketplace are looking at an 8% to 12% annual return on long-term rental property. Let me give you an example of how this works out. Let's say I purchase a property for $120,000. I put a renter into the property and collect $1,000 each month in rent. Each year, I earn $12,000 in rent. That $12,000 is 10% of my $120,000 investment.

What are the secrets to selling a home quickly?

First and foremost, a plan at the time of purchase is what makes a home sell quickly. The day you buy, you need to know what your team needs to do and when it needs to be done. The right team needs to be put into play and activated immediately after the purchase. Since you do not make money until the property is sold, the exit is what you need to be focused on, even before you make your entrance. The speed with which you line up your contractors is going to play a major role in how quickly you will be able to sell that property.

The next important piece to selling a property is pricing. You want to price your property aggressively so that it sells fast. This is where your market research comes into play. Knowing what other properties are selling for (not listing for) will help you set the right price. Don't worry about squeezing out every last penny. Set a price that secures the profit you wanted when you first started the deal and sell it fast to get that profit. You can lose thousands haggling over a hundred dollars.

Finally, once your property is on the market, make sure that you keep the property attractive. Be sure that it is always ready for potential buyers to view. Too many investors make the mistake of neglecting to ensure that the property is frequently checked on and kept up. You never know when your buyer is going to drive by or visit the property. Make sure that it is always ready.

How do you know what to rehab and what to leave alone?

One of the most common mistakes that new investors make is improve and overspend on a property. They come in with a rehab budget of $15,000 and spend $30,000 to $40,000 instead. Then they wonder why the deal went bad!

You need to learn how to say "no" when it comes to additional rehab. And I should point out that the person you will have to say "no" to most frequently is yourself. How do you know what to say no to? You go the marketplace that is in the immediate area of your subject property and look at the houses that have sold. See what their condition and upgrades were when they sold. Then, set your property up to be just slightly better, perhaps with better fixtures, lighting and appliances. Do not include expensive upgrades that will push the rehab costs way up and eat into your profit. You are not going to live there. The market is telling you what is selling. Listen to it. Then, when the buyers visit your property, they will find everything they were looking for plus some extra beautiful touches you put in. This will keep you just above the other properties that are selling.

REAL ESTATE MARKETING TO SELL

How do I create property deal flow?

Easy! You want as many deal-finding sources working for you as possible. I use direct mail pieces. I use multiple real estate agents. I use other investors. I use HUD homes. I use REO homes. I want my team listening for deals from multiple sources so that potential deals can be found in a lot of ways.

First-time investors tend to just focus on one or two sources. I like to have as many sources as I possibly can. I have found that creating relationships with the right people has created more and better deals than any specific strategy that I have employed in the past. Relationships in the marketplace will create more deals than any other strategy will. Make sure that you and your team members are always building relationships.

How do I generate buyer leads?

The majority of the buyer leads I create are from the existing inventory that I have in the market. I put out great properties and buyers come in to see those properties. However, only one buyer can actually have each property. That leaves all of the other buyers hungry for a property that is just as good as the one that they missed out on. Great inventory will bring in streams of buyers. My team keeps in contact with all of the buyers interested in my properties and we contact them when we have a new one available. Put out good product and you will not want for buyers.

Additionally, those who do buy from you will undoubtedly talk to their friends and relatives about the property that they just purchased. When they are happy with what they bought, they will push their network to you. When you put out great product, you naturally draw buyers because of the quality and the work you are known for. The best marketing that you can do to attract potential and future buyers is to ensure that the product you have to sell today is great. The results that you have on display will speak for themselves.

When should I begin to market my rehab? Do you ever market your homes prior to putting them on the market?

I do not like to market my properties until they are 100% complete. There are many reasons for this. One in particular is that I am not a custom homebuilder. If you find a buyer ahead of time, too often they will start asking you to adjust specific things in the house for them. This will not only wreck your timeline, it will also wreck your budget and your profit, as well.

I prefer to complete my vision on the house and then start marketing the property. The analogy I always draw is "going on a date." Before I head out on a date, I want to make sure that I have everything I need and that my date does, as well—lipstick, purse, shoes. I want to head out the door knowing we are 100% ready. That is the same way I approach selling a property. I step foot out the door when I know it is ready to sell.

How do I find wholesale property buyers?

This business, once again, is all about developing and creating relationships. In this case, the relationships you are after are with the real estate agents who are already working with investor buyers. You want to connect with these people who are already seeking out potential investment properties for other investors.

Another strategy I use is going to the auctions. To understand this strategy, all you have to do is think about the buyers at an auction. They are ready to buy. They have cash. They are willing to take risks. They are willing to close quickly. An auction only has so many properties to sell and there are many buyers at auctions who walk away without a property. I talk to them about what I have available. It's a great place to sell wholesale.

Another way to find wholesale buyers is to research the MLS. Look for homes that appear to have been recently remodeled or staged. Then, do some research on who owns the property. You will find patterns in ownership and be able to identify the sales that belong to other investors. Doing a little bit of title research will help you track down those other investors so you can talk to them. If they have bought one property and rehabbed it, the chances of their being willing to buy and rehab another property are very good. I track those buyers down, as well.

WHAT IN THE HECK IS THAT?

What is title insurance?

Title insurance is a policy that protects the lenders when a property is purchased. When a property is being sold, a search is done to ensure that all loans and liens on a property are paid off at or before the sale of the property to a new owner. That is the responsibility of the title company. They do the research to make sure that the property has a clean title at closing. However, things don't always go as planned. This insurance protects the lender in the event that a title issue comes up after the sale of the home. The property buyer typically pays for the title insurance on a property.

What is an HOA?

HOA stands for Home Owners Association. In some areas (usually planned communities and condominium buildings), HOAs are commonplace but they do not exist everywhere. The HOA is responsible for enforcing the rules of a community. They make sure that all properties in their member area are in compliance with all of the codes and regulations established for that community. The HOA is also typically responsible for the maintenance of the common areas in a community (parks, community pools, etc.). Property owners in an area where there is an HOA will pay monthly dues to the HOA, which are used to carry out these tasks.

What is a PUD?

PUD stands for Planned Urban Development. It is the plan for building a community within an urban area. The goal of a PUD is to create a community that is self-sufficient and contains a mix of the different types of properties and amenities that are needed by those who live and work in the community. A PUD will contain plans for office, shopping, residential and recreational spaces.

What is a 1031 exchange?

A 1031 exchange is both a tax strategy and a service provided by specialized companies.

The tax strategy of a 1031 exchange allows property sellers to utilize section 1031 of the U.S. tax code to defer capital gains or losses when they sell a property by purchasing a property of equal or greater value. This is called a "like-kind" exchange.

It can take some time to sell a property and replace it with a like-kind property in proper compliance with the 1031 regulations. In order to facilitate the transactions that accompany a 1031 exchange and to ensure compliance, some companies offer 1031 exchange services.

What is a Self Directed IRA?

A Self Directed IRA (SDIRA) is an IRS-approved vehicle in which you can invest in whatever you want and defer taxes until later or not pay them at all. You can have one or more self directed accounts at the same time—Roth IRA, traditional IRA, SEP IRA, 401(k), etc.

Note that a self directed 401(k) Plan (also known as Indi K or Solo K) is a special type of self directed retirement account. It is the IRS-approved vehicle for self-proprietors and business owners. These plans allow business owners to make larger annual contributions to their retirement accounts and even borrow against the accounts. Unlike other retirement vehicles, there is no income limit restricting the use of a self directed 401(k) plan.

What is infinite banking?

Infinite banking is a term utilized to describe the use of life insurance policies in investment. A whole life policy allows an individual to borrow against monies that have been paid into the policy and earn returns tax-free. Since the process can be repeated multiple times, the use of the money is infinite. The profits returned to such an insurance policy accumulate tax-free. This investment vehicle is favored by investors who want to maintain a greater level of liquidity with their funds while still being able to take advantage of solid investment opportunities.

What is a trust deed?

A trust deed is an investment vehicle in which one can earn passive, monthly, collateralized income. This method of investing has been around for many decades. Like a mortgage, it is a note on a property that is secured by the property itself and guarantees the lender a set interest rate in exchange for the loaned monies.

What is a listing agent?

A listing agent is a real estate agent who represents a seller. They are called listing agents because they list, market and promote properties for their sellers. These agents typically have a lot of active properties they are trying to sell in the marketplace at any given time. Listing agents are good members for your team because their role allows them to come across many potential deals as sellers call on them to list their properties.

What is a buyer's agent?

Simply put, a buyer's agent is one who works with buyers to find properties that meet their criteria. Their clients may be looking for a home to live in or investment properties. This is another group of agents that you want to work very closely with.

There are two primary reasons why you want to work with these agents. They may be working with investors that you can potentially wholesale your properties to even before you complete a rehab. They may also be working with individuals who are looking for a primary residence to live in. They can also bring you buyers for your fully rehabbed properties.

What does it mean to be in the "wholesale" real estate business?

Wholesaling a real estate deal is a term used to describe a transaction in which one individual secures a property with a contract or purchases a property with the intention of selling the property to another party or investor. Sometimes, the individual may assign the contract to the end buyer and take a finder's fee for bringing the investor the deal. Other times, the investor may close the deal and then turn around and sell it to another investor. In this case, the initial investor does not perform the necessary rehab work on the property. It is the investor who buys the flipped property that performs the rehab work and takes the property to market.

What is a home warranty?

A home warranty is a bit of a misnomer. Many people believe that a home warranty will cover all issues that arise with a residential property. In fact, this is not the case. A home warranty is a policy that is typically paid for by the seller of a property and granted to the buyer of the property. While each policy's coverage can vary, a home warranty typically covers the electrical systems, plumbing systems and large appliances that may need repair due to normal wear and tear.

What is a promissory note?

A promissory note is a contract where the borrower promises to adhere to the repayment terms laid out in the contract. It is the borrower's promise to pay the lender as agreed. It is a legally binding contract.

What is a short sale?

A short sale is a transaction in which a bank sells a home to a buyer for an amount that is less than what is owed to the bank. Banks use short sales to minimize or mitigate bad debt that is on their books. For example, $100,000 is owed to a bank on a property at 123 Main Street. The bank is the current owner of the property after a foreclosure that took place on the property. The bank receives an offer from an investor for $80,000 and accepts it. The new buyer purchases the property for $80,000 and the bank accepts the loss of $20,000.

About the Authors

Mike Baird is an international real estate and design educator. He has personally bought and sold over 1,000 homes and owns a large pool of long-term investment properties. He has mentored, motivated and coached thousands of people to create lasting wealth using real estate. Mike is an international reality star and creator of Flip Men which aired nationally and internationally on A&E , Spike, Infinito, and Discovery Networks.

A native of Los Angeles, Mike attended Brigham Young University where he earned his Bachelor's degree from the Marriott School of Management in 2002. Mike is a father of 5, speaks Spanish fluently and enjoys serving in his local community.

He has been written about in USA Today, The Wall Street Journal, The New York Times, and Huffington Post. Mike also contributes regularly to Yahoo Real Estate, AOL, and Realty Trac and Inman News.

Greg Herlean, the best-selling author of *Bank On This*, has spent the last ten years focused on growth opportunities and wealth accumulation through real estate vehicles. He has personally managed over $500 million in real estate transactions. He has flipped 450 homes and 2,000 apartment units. He has also purchased and sold nine hotels.

When he founded Horizon Trust, a New Mexico based custodial company, Greg took his mission of educating Americans on the power of self directed accounts to new heights.

Greg is also a sought-after platform speaker on the topics of estate planning, capital development and investment growth through use of self directed IRA vehicles. These speaking engagements allow him to share his expertise with others who are interested in obtaining greater financial security.

He currently resides in Las Vegas, where he is an active member of the community. Greg is a devoted family man who relishes any opportunity to spend time and enjoy life with his wife, Kristy, and their four beautiful children. Greg is a University of Phoenix graduate with a B.S. in business administration.

Want more Flip, Bank, Live?

You can find more education and strategy from Mike and Greg at FlipBankLive.com

You can also join them on Facebook at:
https://www.facebook.com/wealth4lifeofficial